PUSH THROUGH THE EMOTION

Tips for Managing Emotional Risk

Tonnia Thomas

PUSH THROUGH THE EMOTION

Copyright © 2017 by Tonnia Thomas

All rights reserved. No part of this book may be used or reproduced in any manner whatsoever without written permission except in the case of brief quotations embodied in critical articles or reviews.

Cover design by Ian Heath of West India Design Company

ISBN: 978-0-9988916-0-6

Printed in the United States of America

2017 - First Edition

I dedicate this book to my brother, Terry.
He always had his head buried somewhere in a book;
either reading it or writing it. I bet you are enjoying
heaven with mom and dad.

CONTENTS

Prelude		i
1.	Lost in Emotions	1
2.	Managing Emotional Risk	8
3.	Perspective - What lens are you looking through?	14
4.	Understanding - The WHY to the WHAT	25
5.	Strategic - About Your Response	34
6.	Handle it - Like a Professional	42
7.	Finding Value in Emotions	49
Quotes to Ponder		53
About the Author		54
Acknowledgments		55

PRELUDE

I can come upon you like a locust and make everyone take notice

I can make you feel joy or pain, it's all about how you manage to maintain

I can rob you of a peaceful sleep if you fall for me too deep

I can make you come to the wrong conclusions based on false illusions

I can cause self-doubt rather than encouraging you to figure me out

I can occupy your time by captivating your mind

I can make you stand still against your own will

I can guide your decision making when you are overtaken

I can't always be controlled; so don't make that your goal

I can however be managed if only you knew how;

When I am managed I can be to your advantage here and now

Who am I, you ask

I am EMOTIONS

– Tonnia Thomas

1. LOST IN EMOTIONS

*Human behavior flows from three main
sources: desire, emotion, and
knowledge. – Plato*

We've all heard the saying "women are more emotional than men." First, let me say the premise of this book is not to argue for or against one gender's emotional state, for emotions touch us all throughout our lives regardless of the x or y chromosome. At home, school, work, or play, emotions can touch us on a daily basis, and that is normal. It's not about whether or not we are touched by emotions; it's about what we do with them, how they impact us, and how we play into our emotions (or allow them to drive us) that makes all the difference - especially if an emotion triggers a negative spontaneous feeling.

This is the inspiration that stands behind the writing of this book. I want to help you discover ways to effectively respond to those negative emotions that may catch you off guard from time to time and distract you.

"Lost in Emotion" is a song from the 80s by Lisa Lisa

and Cult Jam. Although the song tells a story about a love interest, a few phrases in the lyrics stood out to me and made me think about the influence our emotions can have on our lives in general, not just in the case of a love interest. For instance, the impact of the emotions she sings about can also be felt when an undesirable experience occurs. Below are a few of the lyrics from the song:

> *I'm lost in emotion*
> *Telling you things you really shouldn't know*
> *Oh baby, I'm lost in emotion*
> *Am I a fool? At least my friends think so...*
>
> *I find myself telling you things*
> *I don't even tell my best friend*
> *I keep showing emotions not knowing*
> *Just where it all stand for us...*
>
> *Hit the beat now (lost)*
> *With my feeling (lost)*
> *I hit the ceiling (lost)*
> *With big emotions (lost)*
> *I can't be dealing (lost)...*

After reading the lyrics more intently, three things resonated with me about the impact of getting lost in negative emotions:

1. We may give power to others to control us when we're lost in negative emotions.
2. When lost in negative emotions, we may be unable to separate personal and business matters.
3. We may suffer consequences when lost in negative emotions.

The power we give others to control us

When we allow negative emotions to influence our actions, we may tell people things they really shouldn't know. "What could that possibly be?" you ask. Perhaps we may reveal a vulnerability, weakness, or things they can use to manipulate us, to throw us off our game, or to lose the focus of our ambition. When others know what makes us tick, they can push our buttons to their own advantage anytime they want. When others learn how to manipulate our emotions (i.e., get you upset, irritated, worried, or frustrated), we give them power to control and distract us. We give them power when we allow our emotions to overtake us and when we react without thinking things through. Do we really want that to happen?

Furthermore, negative emotions rob us of discipline and self-control. When we allow someone else to take control while we are stuck in our emotions, they can reshape our landscape. They can cause us to focus our attention on something that is not the real problem, or they can change the context of the discussion to make us appear a certain way to someone else by pulling us out of our character. If we're not careful, things can shift on us (without our realization that it's happening) while we are buried in our emotions.

We often do not recognize sudden shifts and distractions in our agenda when we are lost in our emotions. Have you ever had a disagreement with someone about one specific thing, but by the time that conversation ended, you had moved on to a different subject without resolving the original issue? Or somehow the spotlight shifted off them and onto you, but you were not sure when or how that happened? It's because they saw a way to distract you and take control of the conversation - perhaps taking the focus and pressure off themselves.

When we are deep into emotions, it may be difficult to catch those sudden shifts and distractions. Keeping a level head (as much as possible), allows us to stay focused on what is important rather than getting distracted by something less valuable. Now, there are times when you may be justified in blowing up, but even then, you have to find a way to regain control and deal with the issue at hand with tact and discretion; this is particularly important in a business setting.

The inability to separate personal and business matters

If we're not careful, our emotions can cause us to get lost in our feelings. Once feelings become entangled with our business dealings, it may be difficult to separate the two, to think clearly, or to see things for what they really are (strictly business and nothing more). This applies to those feel-good emotions as well as those not-so-good emotions.

Separating personal feelings from business can be a difficult thing to do at times, especially when it is your own business. After working with several entrepreneurs, as well as what I've learned from my own experience, I have found a lot of emotions come along with running a business, simply because it is your baby, and no one else is going to care about it the way you do. No one can truly understand the time and energy you invest in it or the sacrifices you've made to keep it going until you find a steady balance. Other business owners may be able to empathize and sympathize with each other, but even then their experiences may differ because their emotions may touch them in a different way or the conditions and circumstances in which they had to operate varied from one person to another.

We make many business decisions daily, and every decision we make can have a significant impact on whether we make it or break it. When we have others depending on us for their well-being or livelihood, it makes it even more nerve-wracking at times. Hence, it is vital for us to take precautions on how we allow emotions to evolve in our business dealings (whether we run our own business or work for someone else). There are times when our intuition will kick in to alert us when something is off during our business dealings; however, I am speaking beyond that scenario.

Now, I am not a psychiatrist; I can only share what I have learned through my own and through others' experiences. One thing I have found to be very valuable in understanding how emotions drive me is knowing when I am being driven by a primary emotion rather than by a secondary emotion. The emotions we display to others are often secondary emotions. The secondary emotion is a symptom of a primary emotion, which is the initial feeling you felt in response to something you experienced.

For example, many people get nervous when they have to speak in public or give a presentation. That nervousness is a secondary emotion to fear. You are nervous because you fear you may forget something, say something wrong, or may not be able to answer a question posed to you; therefore, your fears come through as nervousness. Another example could be the anger you display when betrayed by a close friend, loved one, or confidant in the workplace. The anger is really a secondary emotion; hurt is more likely the primary emotion that turned into anger. Our primary emotions are often overshadowed by secondary emotions because we aren't sure if we want others to know how we really feel, so we often linger and find ourselves stuck in a secondary emotion, sometimes unsure how to come out of it.

Moreover, we must be honest about what triggers our primary emotion to regain control, especially in a professional setting. Is a personal agenda driving your primary emotion, or a legitimate business concern? We must be careful not to allow emotions to make business about our person rather than the real business issue at hand, as we may risk becoming biased or irrational.

The consequences you may suffer

So why should we be concerned about getting lost in negative emotions? Don't we have a right to express or say what we feel? Of course we can say or express what we feel, but there may be consequences that come along with it, depending on how we do it. The consequences of getting lost in negative emotions may include the following:

- Doing or saying something you might later regret
- Fighting the wrong battle because you draw the wrong conclusion and respond based on the conclusion you have drawn through your emotions
- Losing valuable time because you get distracted or take a detour that can stall, delay, or push you off course
- Getting stereotyped by your response because your peers see you in an unfavorable position or out of character
- Losing your control over a situation

So if negative emotions can impair our ability to make decisions, expose things others can use to manipulate us, or cause us to lose control and our creditability, then the inability to manage negative emotions can put us at risk, personally and professionally. Risk can be defined as anything or any situation that exposes someone or something to loss, harm, or danger. For that reason, managing our emotions should be included in our risk management plan for both our personal and business affairs. In the next chapter, we will discuss an approach for managing emotional risk.

2. MANAGING EMOTIONAL RISK

The best way out is always through.
– Robert Frost

Since emotions are a natural part of our being, they have the potential to surface in everything we do (because we carry them with us). The ability to manage our emotions is not only a great asset to have, it also becomes a precious commodity because emotions often play a role in our decision-making process for both our personal and business affairs.

If we think about different types of risk, the source of risk can be segmented into general categories, such as, nature, human error, economic, and speculative risk. We all know humans can make mistakes from time to time, so processes, procedures, and safety programs are put in place to minimize human error. Rarely do you think of someone getting lost in their own emotions as human error, but it does happen from time to time.

So then, how do you manage your emotions? I think it makes sense to handle emotions like any other potential risk to your personal or business affairs, and the first thing you do in risk management is identify what can happen and what could potentially cause the risk to occur. After you identify the risk and its potential causes, you then make a plan to avoid, reduce, or transfer the risk. Because emotions are a part of our human nature, it is difficult to ignore or turn them off 100 percent of the time. Therefore, because you can't completely avoid emotions, you will occasionally encounter them. Consequently, the only thing left to do is to learn how to identify emotional risk then reduce it or transfer it into positive energy instead of feeding into it and getting lost in your emotions.

Step 1. Identifying emotional risk

The first step to managing emotional risk is to recognize when you are in your emotions. After all, you can't address what you don't acknowledge. Knowing when you are in your emotions and what triggers your emotions in a negative way enables you to make a plan to address the issue and govern yourself should it occur. If you think about it, you practice responding to potential risk throughout your life, whether it be at home, school, or work.

For instance, you may have fire drills because someone has identified ways a potential fire can break out. Because there is a potential, once in a while you practice what to do and how to respond in order to avoid casualties and minimize damage to assets susceptible to a fire. By practicing the fire drill, you have a higher probability of everyone getting out safely. After all, we tend to respond better to things we have taken the time to practice and prepare for. If you aren't prepared, anything can happen.

I know you can't prepare for or prevent everything from happening, and yes, even if you prepare, there is still a chance you may not get it exactly right when it occurs. However, acknowledging the risk and conditioning yourself on what to do should the risk occur yields a higher probability of coming out of it more successfully.

So why not take a lesson from that? If you know certain things have the potential to trigger your emotions negatively, identify them and practice what to do in case it happens.

Let's take a moment to identify possible reasons for getting lost in negative emotions. If we are honest with ourselves, many things can cause us to have a negative emotional response, even in business matters. For instance, you may get emotional when unexpected things happen; when you feel what you give out is not being reciprocated back to you; when you venture into the unknown; and when you are treated unfairly, overlooked, embarrassed, underappreciated, or disrespected, to name just a few.

Now, I will be the first to admit that when I felt like I had been overlooked, disrespected, or treated unfairly, that triggered a negative emotion in me. Whenever I am asked to pick an animal that best describes me, I say I am most like a kangaroo. I identify with the kangaroo because of two characteristics: their pouch and their ability to box. Their pouch represents a form of support to me. When we are on the same team, I will do everything in my power to support you, even if I have to pick you up and carry you where you need to be or if I have to pick up an extra load and carry it. However, if you come at me the wrong way (unfairly or unmerited), I will be ready to put up my dukes and go round for round with you - not in a physical way - but I will be ready to defend my point and my rights until you see my point or give up.

What I found was that this often took a lot of time and energy out of me because long after the conversation was over, I would still be thinking about what I should have said and when I should have said it. I lost a lot of time stuck in an emotion. I have learned not everyone and everything is worth that much of my time. I can spend my time and energy on so many other things that can yield a better return on my investment.

Okay, back to possible reasons for negative emotions: Fear can also send us into our emotions. You may fear you are not competent or good enough. You may fear your peers will discover you are not as strong and put together as you appear. Can you think of any others to add to the list?

I want you to take a brief pause to do a quick exercise. Using the table in the Identifying Emotional Triggers exercise at the end of this chapter, take a moment to list the things that have captured you in negative emotions in the past. Also, go back and recall the primary and secondary emotions you felt when that situation occurred.

Now that you have identified what can trigger your emotions, how would you say you have responded in the past to those triggers? Regardless of your answer, let's discuss a way to reduce and/or transfer the impact of negative emotions when they are triggered.

Step 2: Make a plan to reduce or transfer your emotions

Having the capacity to reduce or transfer a negative emotion after you have acknowledged its presence enables you to push through it so that you can come out of your negative emotion as quickly as possible. Note, I said PUSH through the emotion, not ignore it or act like you are immune to it, but PUSH through the emotion. So the magic question now is "How do you PUSH through an emotion?"

You PUSH through emotions by having the capacity to

quickly gain **p**erspective and **u**nderstanding, then **s**trategize and **h**andle your response like the professional you are.

Sounds simple, right? But what does that really mean? Over the next few chapters we will explore the importance of looking at your situation from the right <u>perspective</u> to gain <u>understanding</u> on why it is occurring so that you can be <u>strategic</u> about how to <u>handle</u> your response to the emotion that has been triggered inside you.

Identifying Emotional Triggers

List previous experiences that triggered a negative emotional response from you. What were the primary and secondary emotions you encountered during that experience?

Experiences that triggered a negative emotional response	Primary Emotion	Secondary Emotion

Also, ask your family, friends, or a trusted advisor to recall an instance where you may have displayed a negative emotion, then list the experience below. What triggered the emotion? Sometimes those close to you know what to avoid saying or doing around you if they don't want to trigger a negative response.

3. PERSPECTIVE - WHAT LENS ARE YOU LOOKING THROUGH?

Change your thoughts, and you can change your world. – Norman Vincent Peale

When I was in high school, a quote I found on a calendar has stuck with me throughout my professional and personal development: "You can't see the picture when you are inside the frame." I have found this to be so true. When someone is taking your picture, you really don't know what you look like the moment the picture is taken: you may be smiling, you may have a crazy look on your face, your eyes may be closed because you blinked the instant the picture was snapped, or something could be out of place around you - I think you get my point. It's only after the picture is taken and you look back on it that you realize what you really looked like.

I think not being able to see the picture when you are

inside the frame is synonymous with the idea that it is much easier to give good advice to someone else than to yourself. For some reason, perspective comes into play much clearer when you are dealing with someone else's situation rather than your own. This leads me to believe that if you take your situation, remove yourself as the main character in the scene, and place someone else in the picture frame, you may be able to come up with better advice to give to yourself during trying experiences.

Your experiences can shape you and grow you; it's all about how you look at them. With that said, we now come to the first step of pushing through emotions: Perspective. Your perspective can stunt your growth or stimulate your growth. Gaining the right perspective is about your perception - your point of view.

As I think about the phrase "point of view," I think about glasses. Glasses are made with various types of prescriptive lenses - photochromic, polarized, high-index, bifocals, trifocals, or progressive. Regardless of the lens type, they all serve a common purpose: to correct an individual's impaired vision or to fix their distorted focus from their point of view. Just as the right lens can put things in focus for you, the wrong lens can distort your vision, making things look worse than they really are. Even if you have 20/20 vision, your vision can become impaired if you look through the wrong lens.

Have you ever put on a pair of glasses that weren't meant for you to wear? It distorted your vision, right? Well, did you know that some of your emotions can knock your focus out of whack and distort your vision in the same manner when your emotions are not managed properly? You may not see things correctly or for what they truly are when you are lost in your emotions. The emotional lens you use to size up a situation may be distorting what's right in front of you and causing you to respond incorrectly. The way you see affects how you will be. So how do you see? Are you looking through the right lens when your emotions get triggered? Let's take a moment to discuss the various types of emotional lenses you may be putting on when your emotions are running high to see what we can decipher about how you may be viewing things at times.

Consider the types of lenses mentioned earlier: polarized, photochromic, high-index, bifocals, trifocals, or progressive. I think if you can understand the need for some of these lenses, it may shed some light on why you may view things the way you do.

Photochromic Lens

A photochromic lens automatically darkens when exposed to sunlight. Hmm ... what might you want to darken when it is sitting in the glare of a spotlight? Perhaps a photochromic lens is something you automatically look through whenever a concern arises about your deficiencies, something you may lack and need to improve upon (whether that be lack of competencies, lack of processes, lack of foresight, etc.). If we are honest with ourselves, this is something that can make us uncomfortable and trigger our emotions, especially when it is exposed in a public setting.

When accusations are linked to our deficiencies or embarrassment and humiliation occurs in front of others, we may naturally go into a defensive mode. On the other hand, when something keeps happening and you are the only common denominator in each case, you have to take a step back and ask, "Am I missing something? Does something need to be done differently? Is there something about the process that allows this thing to keep happening?"

In general, I think we have a natural tendency to look externally first rather than internally - "What is it that someone is doing to me?" rather than "What am I doing to myself?" Just as we have gifts that we excel in, we (as human beings) also have limitations, which we generally do not wish to be exposed to others. Sometimes our emotions may distort our point of view because we can't be honest with ourselves about our shortcomings. Perhaps, this may be why we focus on the wrong thing at times - because we don't want to focus internally.

Polarized Lens

Polarized lenses reduce glare reflected off surfaces, making images appear sharper and clearer. When I think about this, I think about how the glare can be so bright that it obstructs my ability to view the entire picture in front of me. Sometimes I have to put my hand up to block sunrays when I am driving, or if I am driving behind another car and the rays from the sun hit a reflective surface on the other car, there is a brightness that may grab my attention and I have to look away from it to get a better view of what's in front of me. If I focus on the glare, I may have an accident because it distorts my vision. So what is that thing that often tries to grab your attention, that thing you simply need to turn away from and block out so that you can see more clearly?

I would venture to say that we often reflect on things that have "happened to me" rather than things that "happened for me." Negative feelings are more likely to be associated with "happened to me," while "happened for me" often indicates a positive outcome or output associated with the experience. Negative emotions can block you from seeing the lesson that was supposed to be learned. They can cause you to give up after a failure rather than to be persistent, based on lessons you learned that have been framed by a new mind-set. They may also block you from even trying it again with a new character because of what you experienced when someone else played the co-starring role.

The best thing you can do for yourself when you go back and reflect on something is to see it from the perspective of what "happened for me" (for your good) rather than what "happened to me." When you focus on what "happened for me," you use your emotional polarized lens to give yourself better clarity and improve your vision so that you can continue to move forward and not get blocked by the glare of the rays from past hurts and bad experiences.

High-Index Lens

A high-index lens is basically a high-tech plastic lens for people with stronger prescriptions. Even though a prescription may be stronger with a high-index lens, one's vision can be corrected with less material, thereby making the lens much thinner. So what is it that you may need to give less weight to but still maintain strength in? Perhaps the high-index lens is what you should be using to view yourself.

Sometimes we just give too much weight to others' opinions, to their definition of who we are and what we can do, rather than knowing who we are. We accept other people's perspectives rather than develop our own. Before you accept others' opinions of you, you should weigh their perspective against their intentions. Is it constructive criticism? Are they genuinely trying to help you grow and achieve your goals? Or are they trying to make you be who they want you to be and do what they want you to do? If it is the latter, you need to reduce the weight on your lens and find strength within yourself. Your strength lies more in how you see yourself and knowing that you are capable of handling whatever comes your way.

In contrast, sometimes the heaviest weight on our emotional lens comes from within. This could be the weight you put on yourself for not knowing what you didn't know, or for a failure you experienced when you made the wrong decision. If this is the case for you, you must learn how to chalk it up to a lesson well learned. Don't continue to carry that weight of guilt, shame, or regret on your lens. Lighten the weight on how you view yourself, and regain your strength so that you can keep pressing forward.

Bifocal/Trifocal Lens

Glasses with bifocal or trifocal lenses serve a purpose too. Bifocal lenses combine vision correction for near-sighted and far-sightedness, with the top of the lens for distance viewing and the bottom for close-up viewing, yet there is a hard line that separates one's ability to see far or near with the bifocal lens. With that in mind, perhaps we see things from only one of two perspectives at any given time. An image is black or white; it has no grey areas (i.e., you either win or lose). Or perhaps you can only focus by zooming in and zooming out from a specific viewpoint, which may cause you to only focus internally or externally (it's about you or the other person). Either way, always going to one extreme doesn't leave room for compromising or for seeing things that may fall in between those two extremes. Hence, your inability to be flexible on your viewpoint may limit or hinder your perspective.

Trifocal lenses, on the other hand, take the bifocal lens one step further by adding a section for people who need help seeing objects that are within a couple feet or so.

Trifocals still have distinctive lines like bifocals, but the magnifying power of trifocals adds to one's range of viewing. So trifocals may be similar to opening your mind to see not only from your own viewpoint but from others' as well, perhaps even enabling you to see a mutual advantage point (i.e., seeing from a point of view that works for all parties involved at some point in time - a win-win).

When you are caught up in your emotions, you may make the mistake of putting on your emotional bifocals rather than your trifocals. In essence, this distorts anything in between for compromise. Is it really only about you or the other person, or is it a combination of the two?

As a case in point, I was speaking to a group of entrepreneurs, and we were discussing ways to optimize business opportunities and increase exposure when you are in the early stages of start-up. The topic of white labeling came up and how sometimes you may have to wear someone else's brand to learn the ropes or gain access or exposure to your target clientele.

At this time, one entrepreneur spoke up and said she had tried that but had a bad experience. She said at one point she was working with a seasoned vet in her industry; however, she couldn't promote herself with the customers she engaged with when working for the seasoned vet, the seasoned vet never gave her credit for any of the work she did, and she had mixed feelings about that.

The first thing I said to her was, "Come out of your emotions; that was simply business." Then another young lady said, "Yeah, she was protecting her business." Guess what? She was correct. The seasoned vet was protecting the portfolio of clientele she had worked hard to build up, and she was very upfront and clear with her about what she could or could not do when engaging with her clientele.

Next, I told the young entrepreneur, "Perhaps you went through that experience so you would know what to do when you expand your business and need to bring on help."

Often you must stop and check the lens you are using to view a situation. Everything isn't always about you or someone mistreating you. Perhaps there is a lesson for you to grasp and use as you continue to grow personally and professionally.

Progressive Lens

Lastly, the progressive lens has a smooth progression of power, enabling the wearer to see at an intermediate distance as well as near and far. Unlike typical bifocals and trifocals, a progressive lens doesn't have lines separating the sections (hence, no hard boundaries to cross over). I would argue that the progressive lens represents where you ultimately want to be when it comes to gaining the right perspective of a situation you may be experiencing - being able to see clearly everything coming toward you (the good, the bad, and the ugly that trigger your emotions) and still manage to keep your composure. Also, you want to be able to see beyond just the moment you are currently in; you want to see the implications that may follow (i.e., not only what is near, but the intermediate and far distances as well). With the progressive lens, you have a higher probability of recognizing and smoothly transitioning out of your emotions to see an issue from multiple angles and then make a rational plan for how to address it. As they say, take the lemons and make lemonade.

Now, after reviewing the purpose for various types of lenses, do you understand how your perspective can influence your emotions and reactions? Did you recognize a pair of lenses that you may be putting on often? Better yet, did you identify a pair of emotional lenses you may need to put on or take off in order to manage your emotions better and maintain the right perspective? To practice seeing through the right lens, complete the Gain Perspective exercise at the end of this chapter.

Opening yourself up to see from the right angle or to broaden your viewpoint is just the first step in pushing through emotions. Next, you must ensure you are interpreting the things you see correctly by gaining understanding. Pushing through emotions will require you to look deeper than just what's on the surface. It will require you to find the WHY to the WHAT. When you discover the WHY, not only will you discover the reason or purpose for the WHAT, you will also unlock the wisdom hidden in you (why).

Think about an iceberg. There is more to the structure than what meets the eye. If you are not careful, what is below the surface can cause major - or even permanent - damage to your vessel. It's the same with emotions: what's hiding deep below the surface of an emotion can cause damage if you don't get to the root cause of it. When you are lost in a negative emotion, you can't see everything as it really is. You have to look beyond the surface to protect yourself from things that may have negative consequences or cause permanent damage.

Gaining Perspective

Sometimes seeing things in terms of what "happened for me" vs. what "happened to me" can give you a broader perspective to an experience you may have encountered. In other words, "What did I gain from the experience?" versus "What did I lose?"

Can you think of something that happened to you that has negative emotions attached to it? This would be something that draws negative energy to you every time you reflect on it. On the other hand, is there something you want to get over that has been difficult to move forward from? List the experience below, then answer as many of the following questions as possible.

List a prior experience that draws negative emotions to you:

Because I experienced that,	What happened for me?
I learned >	
I met or was exposed to >	
I no longer >	
I started >	
I have a process or procedure for >	

Perspective

After reviewing the list, would you say it caused you to grow in some aspect? Do you have a new perspective on the experience?

4. UNDERSTANDING - THE WHY TO THE WHAT

Life is 10% what happens to me and 90% how I react to it. – Charles R. Swindoll

In Stephen Covey's book *The 7 Habits of Highly Effective People*, he lists Habit #5 as "Seek First to Understand, then to be Understood." Often when we are lost in our emotions, it's typically the other way around: we want to make other people understand us, our actions, our response, and our reasoning. We generally want them to see our way instead of understanding their way or why the situation we are experiencing has occurred in the first place. This type of response can often make us ineffective at pushing through an emotion.

To be effective at understanding, we have to know more than just the WHAT (i.e., what has or is happening). We also need the capacity to recognize and comprehend the WHY linked to the WHAT in order to push through the emotions attached to the WHAT. Many times, we stop at the WHAT of our emotions. We may get to the WHY only after we have allowed the emotions to control us by reacting to the WHAT with an emotional response. I call this the aftershock.

Typically, after we have acted out in our emotions and have been given time to reflect and get over the shock of the unexpected or unwanted, then we get to the point where we seek understanding. However, wouldn't it be great if we could stop in our tracks when our emotions first hit us and try to gain understanding before we react with an emotional response? There is a way to condition yourself to do this.

When I think of someone trying to gain understanding, I think of small kids. When they want to know something or when they don't understand, they will ask you why all day long until they get an answer that satisfies their curiosity. You can be riding in your car, and they will see something that piques their interest and proceed to ask you a question about it. Of course, you give them an answer, and then they follow up with why again, then you have to give them another answer to validate your first. As you know, this game can go on and on until they feel they have a satisfactory answer.

Believe it or not, there are professionals in manufacturing and quality assurance who take on this demeanor of repeatedly asking why to get to the root cause of a nonconformance. They do this by using the Five Whys (5 WHYs), a tool often used in manufacturing and quality assurance for preventative and corrective action analysis to get to the root cause of a problem or nonconformance. Once the root cause is defined, then appropriate measures can be put in place to correct the problem or minimize the occurrence of the nonconformance as much as possible.

Here is how it works. First, you state the problem or concern that has occurred. Next, you ask, "Why is that?"

and then write the best possible answer available to you at the time. Based on the answer, now you ask again, "Why is that?" and you continue to ask this question for at least five (5) times. The notion here is that the root cause of the problem should eventually come to light before or by the time the fifth why is answered. Below is an example of how it could work:

Problem statement: I am frustrated with one of my team members.

   1. Why is that?
   They act like they can't write a proposal.

     2. Why is that?
     They constantly ask me questions.

        3. Why is that?
        They're unsure about rates & other factors.

           4. Why is that?
           They just don't have my tribal knowledge.

               5. Why is that?
               Some say no written protocol or guide.

As you can see in this example, as we went through the 5 WHYs, the focus shifted off an emotional state (which is the WHAT that was of concern) to the root cause of the emotion occurring in the first place: a failure in process and procedures that had not been addressed before.

I have found this tool to be very helpful in pushing through an emotion because as I go deeper into trying to understand the WHY, the effect of the emotions weakens because I start to find *reasoning* for the WHAT rather than *reacting* to the WHAT. Reasoning puts you in a more neutral mind-set, which can help increase receptivity. It takes your focus off the emotion and challenges you to try to find a justification for the WHAT instead of accepting it at face value and reacting.

Sometimes there is a justification for the WHAT that makes the WHAT more acceptable to us, regardless of whether the WHAT is to our liking or not. For instance, if your teenager came home and said they wrecked your car, you may immediately go into your emotions. But if your teenager came home and said, "I was driving down the street and a car was in the wrong lane coming toward me, so I had to pull off the road and I hit a tree which wrecked your car," you would have a different reaction. Yes, your emotions may still kick in out of concern for your child, but it would certainly be to a lesser degree than the first option. Why? Because you know the root cause of the wreck. You know the reason for it, the WHY behind the WHAT. The WHY justified the WHAT, so the intensity of your emotions was reduced because you were given insight into the cause of the wreck (you received understanding and wisdom).

If we seek first to gain understanding before reacting, I think we will see that it will become easier to manage our emotions. I think most of us automatically play the 5 WHATs (not a tool) instead of the 5 WHYs, making us find reasons to react more in our emotions rather than finding a reason for the WHAT. The 5 WHATs basically say, "What else happened?" rather than "Why is that?" which may sound something like the following:

PUSH THROUGH THE EMOTION

Problem statement: My boss canceled my one-on-one meeting.

> **1. What else happened?**
> He said he was going to reschedule but he hasn't.
>
>> **2. What else happened?**
>> He hasn't replied to my emails about taking vacation nor my project feedback.
>>
>>> **3. What else happened?**
>>> My reimbursement form hasn't been signed yet either.
>>>
>>>> **4. What else happened?**
>>>> I saw him talking with Jane during the time we were supposed to be meeting.
>>>>
>>>>> **5. What else happened?**
>>>>> I don't think my boss really cares about me.

Then again, in reality it could actually be something to this effect if the 5 WHYs are asked.

Problem statement: My boss canceled my one-on-one meeting.

> **1. Why is that?**
> He wasn't prepared for the meeting.
>
>> **2. Why is that?**
>> He didn't get a chance to review the emails I sent him.
>>
>>> **3. Why is that?**
>>> He was working with Jane on a presentation.
>>>
>>>> **4. Why is that?**
>>>> He received a last-minute call from his boss requesting information for a meeting tomorrow.
>>>>
>>>>> **5. Why is that?**
>>>>> An investor is in town for a day and he agreed to meet for an overview of a project we are working on.

As you can see, both examples have the same problem statement, but they have totally different end results when asking yourself "Why is that?" vs. "What else happened?" You see, asking "What else happened?" instead of "Why is that?" just drives you deeper into your emotions. As you start recalling all the things that have happened, you can start reminiscing over things that may not have anything to do with the current situation; however, it validates the emotion you are feeling. Next, you start to relive those experiences and how they made you feel. At this point, you are compounding all those emotions on top of each other and getting lost in them again, which makes it harder to see clearly and push yourself out of it. We must be careful not to falsely validate our emotions.

From this point forward, let's make a conscious effort to become effective in understanding others and the WHY that goes with the WHAT. As mentioned previously, it may help to switch roles, put yourself in their shoes, and ask yourself why you would do this if you were them and see what your answer is.

Oftentimes, when unfortunate things happen to us, we are quick to ask "Why me?" We stop at the first why, which may be an emotional state, rather than digging a little deeper to see the true cause or purpose for the situation we are in. Or we get caught up in the 5 WHATs instead of the 5 WHYs. Please refrain from doing the 5 WHATs.

Okay ... some of you may be saying to yourself, "But what if I can't come up with a valid WHY for the WHAT?" To be honest, there will be instances when the WHY can't be revealed to you the way you want it, even when you try to search for it. Some things just happen without any rhyme or reason, and you cannot get stuck there searching for an answer.

In this situation, you may have to define your own

WHY to move forward - look for a positive potential purpose for why the situation you are in occurred. Could it be to grow you or to make you stronger? Did it happen to expose you to something you didn't know or to prepare you for another situation you will discover in the future? Was it necessary to redirect you, or could it be just the thing that needed to happen to push you to the next level? Remember, not every bad experience is there to harm you. It might be to prepare you.

Seeking to Understand

We often react to negative emotions rather than try to reason and understand them, or to understand someone else's actions in a particular situation. Below are some examples of how one may reason rather than react.

Reacting	Reasoning
Don't ever do that again!	Perhaps there is a better way to go about doing this.
What did you just say to me?!	I don't think I fully understood you; could you explain that differently?
So what do you want me to do about it?!	Are there any tips or recommendations you would suggest trying - things that have worked well for you?
Why do I have to keep repeating myself?! Why do we have to keep going over the same thing again and again?	I want to make sure we are understanding each other correctly; can you tell me what I just said and what it means to you?
You never listen to me!	I am not sure if my point came across the way I intended; what did you take from that?
Why did you let that happen?!	How did you come to that result? What drove your decisions?
What were you thinking?! This is crap!	I want to follow your thought progression; walk me through this.

PUSH THROUGH THE EMOTION

To help you with reasoning, try doing the 5 WHYs to get to the root cause of a problem you may be experiencing. First, state the problem, then ask "Why is that?" for each answer you give. Remember to answer "Why is that?" and not "What else happened?"

Problem statement:

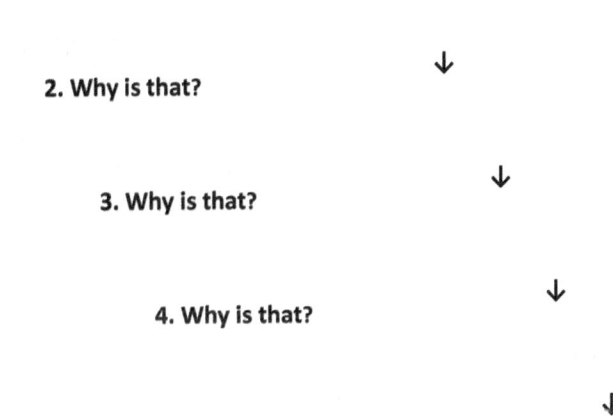

    1. Why is that?

        2. Why is that?

           3. Why is that?

              4. Why is that?

                  5. Why is that?

5. STRATEGIC - ABOUT YOUR RESPONSE

Positive people have negative thoughts, too. They just don't allow those thoughts to grow too big. And they make sure to stop them from following them around all day. – Karen Salmansohn

Feelings are much like waves, we can't stop them from coming, but we can choose which one to surf. – Jonathan Martensson

Now that you have mastered understanding the WHY to the WHAT, you have unlocked wisdom hidden in you. What are you going to do with it? The best thing to do is to think about how to make that wisdom work to your advantage in a positive light. In other words, be strategic about your next response instead of just reacting.

You have to be strategic about how you spend your

time because there is only so much time in one day, and once it is lost, you can't get it back. This should move you to put measures in place to practice managing emotional risk because emotions can interrupt your thought process and paralyze you for the rest of the day (valuable time you can't get back).

Whenever you find yourself in this emotional state, before you make another move, you have to take a time-out (whether it's an internal mental break or physical activity) to reevaluate, regroup, and reposition yourself from where you are. Whenever I need to take a time-out from my thoughts, I play Panda Pop, a game I discovered on my phone when I was waiting at an airport one day. Little did I know at that time that the game would become a tool I would often use to clear my mind and refocus my thoughts.

The whole objective of the game is to free all the baby pandas stuck in bubbles before you run out of the balls used to pop the bubbles. When I first started playing the game, I was trying to pop every single bubble in sight, but then I learned I didn't have to pop each individual bubble; I had to be strategic about how to use the tools in the game to clear multiple bubbles with one ball. The game required me to strategize to win and go to the next level. After so many levels, a new caveat is always thrown into the picture, which causes me to strategize more about how to use the tools I have to free all the baby pandas.

It's a fun game (and they keep adding new levels - fun, fun, fun), but more importantly, this little game has done wonders to help me re-center and neutralize my thoughts when my emotions are triggered or when I just need a clear mind. When I am strategizing how to clear the board and win, nothing else matters at that time. Also, I never buy extra balls to win the game. Once I use up all my free lives,

Strategic

I simply wait a few minutes for the game to reset. This forces me to strategize more.

If you think about it, some of the highest-paid professionals in the world are always calling time-outs to strategize their next move. Do you ever pay attention to the coaches at a professional football game? They collect information about their team and their opponent's capability throughout the game. Depending on their situation (their position, what yard line they are on, their score, the time left in the game, players on the field, etc.), they devise a plan to help position their team to win. You are the coach, so take a step back, evaluate your position, and devise a plan from a positive advantage point.

This is not to say you let someone take advantage of you. Be smart and approach it in such a way that someone doesn't stereotype you or cancel you out because they feel you can't handle pressure or a difficult situation. Remember, be strategic and keep your power. You simply have to ask yourself what is there to gain or lose. You have to consider the goals you want to achieve and the impact your response will have on your ability to achieve the goals you set for yourself both personally and professionally. If the current circumstance can have an impact on your ability to achieve your goals, then think about how to regroup to get back on track from where you are. If there is nothing impinging on your morals and values or to bring you closer to achieving your goals in the next action you are thinking about taking, then you may want to reconsider your actions. Focus your energy someplace more positive.

To be strategic also means to have the right intentions and the right approach when it comes to your response. The right intention would be thinking about what's the next best action for the parties involved without compromising your morals and values. The right approach would be the delivery method that you use to allow others to receive your message as it was intended to be received. Sometimes we have the right intentions but the wrong approach with our response.

Your tone and demeanor can push someone away or toward you. I have always said you can tell anybody anything you want them to know; it's all about how you say it. You can tell a person whatever you need them to know without degrading or belittling them. I tried hard to get this idea through to a colleague I once had who thought that being stern and rigid all the time (and sometimes downright insulting) would make people follow suit. I often said, "Right message, wrong approach." No one wants to be talked down to.

A strategic response attacks the problem not the person. When you attack the person and not the problem, you distort your message and now it can't be received as intended. Ears get clogged, and they stop listening and start defending. When things get personal, it is easier to trigger emotions. Just because you can respond to personal attacks a certain way doesn't mean someone else will. We make the mistake of thinking everyone processes things the same way; they don't. One size doesn't fit all, so you may have to alter your approach to get your point across instead of having a one-size-fits-all mentality. People have different personalities. You have to find ways to reach different people with the same message.

Now with all that said, are you ready to respond? What are you using to make decisions - feelings, strategy, purpose, or what? Always consider the consequences of your actions (long-term/short-term). Before responding, ask yourself, "Do I have the right intention and approach, or am I just reacting? Am I attacking the person or the problem?" The next time you find yourself in an emotional state, call a time-out (play Panda Pop if you have to) and practice devising a strategic response by completing the Strategizing to Win activity at the end of this chapter.

Strategizing to Win

Being strategic about your response means looking for the best course of action that will get you another step closer to achieving your ultimate goal. Sometimes responding out of negative emotions can push you a step back or paralyze you in your tracks. Take a moment to think about what the next best move is for you or your business. Sometimes you may need to purge yourself of the initial feelings and emotions in order to think strategically.

Follow the instructions below to devise a plan to win.
1. Below, write your current situation.
2. In the following table, write the thing you feel like doing the most, regardless of the consequences, in the column titled "What do I feel like doing?" Get your feelings off your chest.
3. Think about the goals and objectives you want to achieve. In the next column, write the response that would be best for your situation and still keep you on track to achieving your goals and/or objectives.
4. Answer the questions honestly under the "My Game Plan" column for each scenario.

My Situation:

Strategic

My Game Plan After listing your response to the two scenarios, answer the questions in this column for each scenario.	What do I feel like doing the most?	Best approach to achieve my goals and objectives?
Am I attacking the person or the problem with this approach?		
Will this really help me win or just make me feel better about the situation?		
What outcome am I expecting as a result of my response?		
How will this help me? Where may it lead me?		
Is it worth the risk? (y/n)		

Below are examples of attacking the problem vs. attacking the person.

Attacking the Person	Attacking the Problem
You always get this wrong.	Let's go through this together and figure out why this error keeps occurring.
You missed the deadline; that cost us big-time.	Was the time allotted adequate for the amount of work required? Did we have the proper resources in place to make this happen? Did everyone get a scope of work? Did something unexpected happen?
Your department is slow. Your people need to pick up their pace.	Is there something causing a bottleneck in this area? Is the workload proportional to the resources? What's the typical turnaround?
You sent the wrong package to the client; this can't happen again.	Was an order confirmation sent to the client? Were the boxes labeled correctly? Did the driver get the correct paperwork?
I should have known you wouldn't get it right; you are too green.	Were expectations, outputs, and outcomes clearly defined and written?

6. HANDLE IT - LIKE A PROFESSIONAL

Keep calm and carry on. – Ministry of Information

Strategizing helps you develop a plan to handle a situation properly. However, you also want to make sure you always have a grip on your mannerisms to execute your plan with professionalism and not emotions. Therefore, maintaining composure as you execute is important.

I was having a conversation with two ladies some time ago, and one lady made a comment about a particular subject in which I thought I had given a neutral response. I immediately found out my response wasn't neutral at all because the lady said to me, "It's all in yours eyes. You don't have to say a word. You talk with your eyes."

You see, your words aren't the only way you show emotions; your composure and body language do too, so you have to remember to remain poised when giving your response - put on your poker face. Remember, poker is about convincing the other players you have the best hand without revealing what you are really holding, which is relatively the same as keeping your composure without revealing how you really feel. This can work both ways - not showing you are really hungry for a deal or not showing you are about to blow a fuse.

For example, an entrepreneur was sharing an experience she had with a caller while starting up a restaurant with her husband. An individual called and said, "Hey, I can help you get at least forty more sales each week, but I want in on some of the profit." The owner said to herself, "I don't know this person or what they are about," so she politely said, "We aren't interested in doing that at this time, but perhaps an opportunity may arise in the future." The caller then proceeded to say okay and asked if she did the cooking. The entrepreneur said no, that her husband did the cooking. The caller then insisted on speaking to him. The business owner said, "My husband does the cooking. I run the business," and politely said again, "I will be happy to let you know if an opportunity comes up for us to look at a support model such as this."

The owner said that although she felt like she wanted to go through the phone and grab the caller, she decided she couldn't let that come across in her tone of voice. She managed not to respond in her emotions mainly because she didn't know this person or who they knew, and she didn't want to take a chance on anyone smearing their business.

You see, she handled the situation professionally regardless of how she really felt because she thought about the impact a negative response could have on her business. This is what you must do: think about the impact your response can have and handle your response like a professional. You never know who will hear about how you responded to an experience. Practice handling your response like a professional by considering some of the questions outlined in the Handle It exercise at the end of this chapter.

Sometimes wearing a uniform reminds us to keep our composure when on the clock. When you are in uniform, you take extra precautions when it comes to handling yourself with other people because whatever you do is not just a representation of you, but a representation of the brand image you may be sporting at that time. Even if your emotions start to kick in, you tend to resist the urge to let them control you a little more while you have that uniform on, but once it comes off, it can be a different story.

An example of this is the character Tom Hanks played in the movie *The Green Mile* with Michael Clarke Duncan. In this movie, Tom played the head prison guard on death row. There were basically two sides to him in the movie, one that could empathize and sympathize with the prisoners and one that could command authority and perform his job without being fazed. If I am not mistaken, I remember seeing a review about the movie that talked about these two sides of his character. The review spoke to how his hat may have been a symbol that signified how he responded to the prisoners. When he approached a prisoner's cell without the hat, that was when he empathized with them the most. When he wore the hat to their cells, it tended to be strictly business with little room for emotions. Perhaps we can learn a thing or two from this.

Well, what do you do when the uniform you put on each day to conduct business is just you? What do you put on to guard yourself from playing into negative emotions so that you can handle business as a professional, as if you were representing a big brand? The truth is, you are representing a huge brand - your own. Can you identify a prop or a code word that sets the tone for how you should approach a situation - something to remind you to separate a personal response from a professional response? When you know you are walking into a situation or dealing with someone that has the potential to put you in an emotional state (especially when family and/or friends are a part of the business, which I will come back to shortly), find something that can serve as a cue to keep it professional. Another option is to put on some fake reading glasses as a reminder to see things through your emotional progressive lens (as we talked about in chapter 2).

If a prop or code word doesn't work for you, perhaps relating to a character will - for instance, Phylicia Rashad's character Clair Huxtable on *The Cosby Show*. If you study her character, she often kept her composure in pretty much any situation or environment. Whether dealing with a client at work or her family at home, she was the epitome of professionalism. She knew how to transition in and out of her emotions so calmly and smoothly.

In an interview with Oprah, Beyoncé once said that she transforms into her Sasha Fierce personality when she hits the stage because it allows her to perform and get the job done confidently and fearlessly. No one knew she was putting on that character until she revealed it in her interview. Note, during her performances, only she knew she was putting on Sasha Fierce; everyone else just saw Beyoncé performing. What can you put on internally as a uniform or personal protective equipment to help you get the job done with professionalism and to minimize the triggers that can cause you to respond in negative emotions?

Now ... back to family and friends in business. I have had the opportunity to work with several business owners that have personal relationships involved in their business operations in one form or another. No matter if it is a husband/wife team, sister/brother, parent/child, friends, or a dating couple, the potential to be touched by emotions are magnified tenfold when dealing with personal relationships in business because you tend to accept and tolerate behavior from personal relationships that you wouldn't dare put up with if it was someone else. In this case, not only are you dealing with people that you care about (that has an emotional component all by itself), but when you add business matters on top of that, it just compounds the degree and frequency to which emotions have the potential to overtake you. If you are not careful, you will be compounding emotions like compounding interest on money you owe to the IRS. This is not to say don't do business with someone with whom you have a personal relationship, but be aware that it can be just as emotionally stressful at times as it is enjoyable.

Remember to keep it professional. Handle your family and friends like you would any other business partner, employee, contractor, or client. If they are your clients, then give them proposals, contract agreements, invoices, payment terms, thank-you notes, and courtesy just as you would any other customer. If you are working as partners or as their employer, then put the working relationship in writing: outline your ownership, roles, and responsibilities, as well as your boundaries for doing business together. The worst thing you could do is to betray or break the respect and trust you have for each other. Once that is broken, it's hard to get it back. Emotions will be high while at work, and then you take them home with you for the evening.

Don't leave yourself open to be touched by negative emotions on a regular basis; put safeguards in place to keep business relationships from going down personal boulevards. Just as you should keep your personal financials separated from your business dealings, put precautions in place to keep it professional as much as possible. Choose who you bring into your business wisely and know your boundaries for doing business.

Also, be aware of each other's strengths and limitations - particularly the limitations because this is what will irk you and work your nerves. Once you have recognized their limitations, decide whether to accept them with their limitations and find ways to work around it or whether to properly remove them from the process if a more suitable role is not available for them to play. If you are a personality type that will conduct business by any means necessary to get what you want, then don't involve personal relationships in your business because you will stay on an emotional roller coaster. Moreover, such involvement could result in the demise of both your relationship and business.

Handle It

Making sure the message you want to deliver comes across to the receiver as intended will require understanding your audience as well as delivering the message in a professional manner. Consider the following to help you process your thoughts before executing your game plan.

What message do I want to get across to my audience? (Keep it concise and to the point.)
What approach can I use to deliver the message in a professional manner/setting?
Things I may want to avoid saying or doing to ensure my message doesn't get distorted when I deliver it (e.g., facial expressions, body language, innuendo, etc.):

7. FINDING VALUE IN EMOTIONS

Strive not to be a success, but rather to be of value. – Albert Einstein

Until this point, we have focused on emotions in terms of risk management, but before we depart, I have one last word to say about emotions. I want to make sure you realize that there is a way to benefit from emotions as well. If you think about it, there is an appropriate place to engulf yourself in emotions, especially in business. Where is that? Drumroll, please … it's when you discover how your talent, skills, or service offerings can become a solution for an unmet need for your target audience. Wait - before you say anything, I'm not finished yet.

This is important because emotions are usually behind unmet needs. I will say it again: typically behind an unmet need is an emotion that an individual is trying to fulfill or satisfy. Once you identify that unmet need and the emotion associated with it, you are able to captivate and touch your target audience by speaking to them in terms of the emotional need they desire to satisfy, which can present opportunities for you to generate revenue. How is that?

Well, think about why people buy a good or service. They buy because what they purchase gives them something in return. In other words, people actually buy *solutions* not *products*. But we often make the mistake of selling a specific item versus the solution that is gained via the good or service. People buy because it may help them do a job, solve a problem, or address a pain point or a frustration. It may even bring them some type of pleasure or entertainment. Then again, perhaps they buy because it's the only or best option they have at the time to help them do one of the things above. Regardless which reason applies, there is an emotion behind it when dealing with a consumer. For instance, I may buy a good or service because it makes me feel or look smart or feel safe; perhaps it builds my confidence or makes me feel sexy when I put it on; maybe it helps me feel healthy or happy because I can bring a smile to someone else's face with it.

With that said, if you have to spend time engulfed in emotions, focus your time on understanding how your target audience can use your talent, skills, or service offerings to satisfy one of their emotional needs. If you know the answer to that question, then you have just discovered value. This, my friend, is where spending time in emotions is beneficial and strategic for your career or your business. Spend your time on something that can give you a payback rather spending your time paying someone back (reacting to what someone did or said to you).

After being exposed to several business owners - regardless of the business industry or whether the business was merely a vision or a company that has been fully up and running for many years - the one thing all of them ponder, at one time or another, is how to continue building revenue to maintain and grow their business. This is an important question to answer because without a demand for their service and a strategy to continuously breathe life into their business, it will eventually die.

The answer is in the emotion associated with the unmet need. Value is gained when filling an unmet need. Also, remember that value is subjective and given by the customer. You have to think in terms of value from your target audience's perspective, not your own. Many times we make the mistake of selling the value of our service offerings in terms of what we think is valuable versus how the customer may define value.

Now, you may be wondering how you get to the unmet need or the emotion behind an unmet need. I'm going to touch on this briefly because this subject is in a class all by itself.

A basic way to recognize need is to simply ask. Your target audience can tell you their needs through surveys, in-depth interviews, focus groups, and even customer complaints. However, one thing you want to be aware of is that your target audience may not be able to articulate all their needs to you in spoken words. One reason is that they may not be fully aware a need exists or that a solution could be developed to address their need. Some of their needs are communicated through their compensated behavior (i.e., things they do to supplement or make up for something that is missing, that doesn't work well, or that is poorly designed).

When one can't articulate a need in words, you may be able to recognize it by taking time to study and observe their actions to gain insight into their need. What are those intentional or unconscious things they do to change the form or use of a product? What are they doing or using to help them do a job or perform a task?

Once you identify a compensated behavior, you should then question why they behave in that manner. You could ask them directly and/or go back to a tool we discussed earlier - the 5 WHYs. State the problem or behavior you observed and ask "why" repeatedly to get to the root cause and the emotion behind their need to act in their compensated behavior.

Remember, value is found when you can provide a solution to fulfill a need your target audience has (spoken or unspoken). Before you can recommend a solution, you must first know and understand their needs and the emotions that drive them. When you identify the unmet need and the emotion that drives it, you find the value.

Valuing Emotions

As our time together draws to an end, my hope is that this book has enabled you to gain a fresh perspective and some insight into the benefits of understanding emotions. Whether you are trying to minimize your risk to your own emotions or trying to find the unmet need associated with others' emotions, both have value. If for no other reason, I hope you continue to invest in yourself to minimize your risk for human error by becoming effective in pushing through your emotions. Remember to PUSH through. Don't try to ignore them or act like you don't feel them. Whenever you find yourself in negative emotions, acknowledge it. Then remember to take a time-out to ensure you have the right perspective and challenge yourself to gain understanding. After you unlock the wisdom, strategize a game plan to win, and then handle your response like the professional you are. I know you can do it. Don't forget to put on your progressive lens.

QUOTES TO PONDER

A big part of emotional intelligence is being able to feel an emotion without having to act on it. - Anonymous

What you do speaks so loudly that I cannot hear what you say. - Ralph Waldo Emerson

The mind is everything. What you think you become. - Buddha

I don't want to be at the mercy of my emotions. I want to use them, to enjoy them, and to dominate them. - Oscar Wilde, *The Picture of Dorian Gray*

Never react emotionally to criticism. Analyze yourself to determine whether it is justified. If it is, correct yourself. Otherwise, go on about your business. - Norman Vincent Peale

Don't mix bad words with your bad mood. You'll have many opportunities to change your mood, but you'll never get the opportunity to replace the words you spoke. - Anonymous

In the middle of difficulty lies opportunity. - Albert Einstein

When people hurt you over and over, think of them like sandpaper. They may scratch and hurt you a bit, but in the end, you end up polished and they end up useless. - Chris Colfer

Nothing is impossible; the word itself says 'I'm possible.' - Audrey Hepburn

ABOUT THE AUTHOR

In one word, Tonnia is a builder. While she's not building real estate, she is intentional about building programs, processes, and systems to help others build a foundation and structure for growing to their next level. Helping others live out their dreams and bringing their visions to life is like erecting a new building or refurbishing an old one in Tonnia's eyes. This is her construction. Whether through her own consulting business, teaching classes at the Women's Business Center of Charlotte, or special program initiatives offered via her nonprofit, Training to Work an Industry Niche (TWIN), Tonnia is passionate about supporting and promoting the professional development of individuals on three levels: workforce development, youth career development, and small business development.

Did you find the tools in this book helpful?

Would you like to have spare worksheets in your toolbox to use whenever you need them? Visit www.tonniathomas.com to download a free *Push Through the Emotion Workbook*.

ACKNOWLEDGMENTS

To my brothers and sisters, Ben, Ann, Pat, Vickie, Cathy, Gail, Annette, Faye, Daryl, Chenequia, Tony, and Marceda (my best friend who is like a sister), thank you for your love, support, and encouragement. You have always been there whenever I needed you. I could not ask for better siblings than you.

To my Bible study group, thank you for your prayers and providing a venue where we can all share and learn from one another.

www.ingramcontent.com/pod-product-compliance
Lightning Source LLC
LaVergne TN
LVHW041458070426
835507LV00009B/679